Seeing With The Eyes Of The Spirit

Dr. Michelle Davis

This book is a work of Spiritual Education. Unless otherwise noted, the author and the publisher make no explicit guarantees as to the accuracy of the information contained in this book and in some cases; names of people places have been altered to protect their privacy.

First Published for:
Maximize Publishing Inc. 6/19/12 & 4/25/13

ISBN: 978-1-105-87254-9 (PB) lulu

ISBN: 978-1-105-87255-6 (EB) lulu

Maximize Publishing Inc.
ISBN-13: 978-0615809182
ISBN-10: 0615809189

Contents:

Foreword

Dr. Michael A. McCain

First allow me to say that I am humbled to be a part of this celebration of achievement. I call it a celebration because there's a prophetic unction in me that confirms that after this the gift we know as Dr. Michelle Davis is no longer a local gift but a gift being released to nations. The thing I love about books is that they are the tools that reach people in places where your feet can't personally tread. This book will take legs and enter in to homes, offices, libraries, churches, computers, phones and eBook readers. I am ecstatic about the advancement that publishing and media has taken on over the last few years. It makes spreading the Gospel easier and it is as near to us as a text on our phone, an eBook on our kindle or download to our computers. Wow, times have changed.

Speaking of Change, Seeing through the Eyes of The Spirit is a book I deem to have been written straight from the heart to God's people. I believe the mandate that this book has is to redeem the relationship between the sheep and the Shepherds. You need not anyone tell you that the state of the church in this present time is in serious trouble and true leadership and redemption is needed. There's prophetic oil on Dr. Michelle Davis that many leaders and sheep have been gleaning from for years for deliverance, healing and direction.

Part of the assignment with seeing through the eyes of the spirit is to get leaders and local members back on target with God true plan and original purpose for ministry and submission to leadership. Yes, I did say submission! Submission is like a cuss word in Christian circles, because we have a generation of people that are so spoiled with information there under the impression that they can lead themselves rather than allowing Gods plan for leadership to play out in their lives. Let me tell you right now in case you didn't know, God's plan for leadership and submission has not changed! We may have a wiser or smarter generation but our people are still dumb to some things as to how to navigate through that information and take action in their lives.

With that statement in mind, that is the true purpose for leadership and the purpose for why God would give you a pastor, it's to help you navigate through life and reach the bull's eye target of your expected end. Are you ready to grow? Are you ready to be fed? Are you ready for real leadership? Are you ready to unlock your calling, destiny and purpose? Then you have the right book in your hands!

I highly recommend that you read this with some friends, family members. I would even say share this with the leader of your local church. This is a jewel and a blessing to the body of Christ that needs not to be hid. This is the hour to connect with your prophetic mandate and seeing through the eyes of the spirit will help you align yourself with that purpose.

Enjoy!

Why I Wrote This Book:

Dr. Michelle Davis

When embracing the assignment to write *seeing with the eyes of the spirit*, my heart began to go on a quest to answer some of the longing questions I am repeatedly faced with in ministry from both leaders and lay members.

This book is written to speak to all who struggle with understanding **why they must have a shepherd, what is the shepherd's responsibility how should I respond to my leader, and how do I know if I have found my spiritual parents in the Lord?**

Through these words he is ministering directly to you, begin to open up your spirit and receive that you may be in the right connection with the one that is **"SEEING WITH THE EYES OF THE SPIRIT"** for you.

Introduction

The Lord Has called me to be a Shepherd. That means I am called to watch over, protect, lead, guide and feed the sheep. I am also a seer, I see in the spirit realm. Therefore, God had graced me with a gift to SEE with the eyes of the spirit. I am a prophet; God has called me to warn the people of his word. Since becoming a pastor, I have experienced many situations. It is from that very place I am coming to you to pour out the oil of wisdom that God has given me as a Shepherd.

Seeing with the eyes of the Spirit was inspired by seeing that many of us just do not care about our relationship with our leaders, but God spoke to me and said **"speak from my heart, let my sheep know that a new wind is blowing and the next level in their life is based on their relationship with their covering."**

There is one that God has called to see in the spirit for you. God knows the way that you should take but he has sent you a human agent (your pastor) that has his heart and mind to help you get to that appointed place.

As a *pastor*, I say get in your proper fold, love your leader, and allow them to feed you that you may grow. Your submission to your leader determines how the oil of God's blessing will flow in your life. Your leader doesn't need your help; they need your submission, so here is your divine call for you to get in place. Are you ready for the oil?

As a *seer*, I say to you that the body of Christ is ready for a shifting, do not allow any more hindrances or excuses to stop you and let you miss the plan of God for your life. Begin to seek God, for your appointed time is now and destiny is ready to be released over your life.

God is speaking to you, YES YOU!!!

Chapter One:

Why Do I Need A Shepherd?

God strategically set up this relationship so that the Shepherd is to lead the sheep. That means, in order for you to be led by a Shepherd, you have to get behind them. If your leader is in front of you, they will see things before you do in most cases. The problem with ministry today is people would rather lead the Shepherd than follow, which is an example of a relationship that is out of order. When God calls you to a leader your responsibility is to fully submit and allow God to do the rest.

This is the importance of a covering; that a person has been called to cover you, to protect you, and to see for you. Your leader cannot see for you if you are a wondering sheep or a sheep that won't submit. You strain the relationship between you and your leader.

A Shepherd knows his/her sheep. Jesus told Peter "if you love me feed my sheep." It is fair to say that a pastor has to love God first in order to love God's people and to be able to feed them properly. **Whatever you do not love, you are not going to treat properly**.

One story in the bible exemplifies the fact behind the statement that someone always sees what you do not see. In Numbers Chapter 22:23 we find Balaam riding on his donkey and his two servants were with him. The donkey **saw** the angel of the Lord standing in the way with a sword drawn in his hand, the 2nd time the donkey **saw** the angel standing between the vineyards, and the 3rd time the donkey **saw** the angel of the Lord standing in a narrow place.

So three times the donkey saw what neither Balaam nor his two friends could see. The Lord was trying to tell Balaam something but he could not see it, but the donkey saw him (the donkey was carrying Balaam and responsible for getting him to his final destination), but he did not trust the donkey and kept smiting him. This is relative to your relationship with your pastor; he/she is responsible for getting you to your destination in God. So you will have to lay yourself aside and trust that God will show them something that you may not see.

The angel of the Lord opened Balaam's eyes so that he could see. He told Balaam "had it not been for the donkey I would have killed you by now," because God was displeased with Balaam. If it were not for your leaders interceding and seeing with the eyes of the spirit for you, there are some situations you would have not made it through because you did not see it coming.

It is important that you have a pastor, and that you know who your pastor is. If a pastor is truly ordained to be your leader/ pastor and you submitting to them they have the ability to keep afflicting spirits off you. In John 10, Jesus said that the Shepherd has the ability to see the wolf coming to attack the sheep.

The shepherd has a rod and staff to bring correction when needed. People misunderstand that everything your leader is going to say to you will not always make you feel good. Every message you hear preached will not always make you jump and shout. Some messages are to provoke you to change, bring conviction and even to correct wherever error maybe present in your life.

You may feel you don not need to go to a local church to be saved, but you do need a pastor to be fed. TV preachers are good but they do not know your spirit. You may say I get more from the TV preachers that I do when I go to my own church, which is a trick of the enemy. If you know that God has given you a pastor that is where you should be eating the biggest portion of your meals and the TV preachers are the additives. They are supposed to add to your spiritual growth not replace your leader.

We are in a generation and a time were people would rather stay home watching TV preachers throughout the week then to step foot in a local assembly. While I am not preaching against the ministry of the TV preachers I want you to understand and know that they are only a supplement to the spiritual nutrients you should already be gleaning from your local pastor. Don't let the devil trip you out and make you miss your deliverance making you believe that you can stay home and self medicate yourself by watching preachers on TV in the comfort of your home.

A Shepherd knows his/her sheep. Jesus said my sheep hear my voice and a stranger they will not follow. Shepherds have the authority to cover you in the spirit, and to speak into your life. They have the authority to help birth you out in the spirit. They are the watchman over your souls and have to account for it before God. You have to allow someone to be your Shepherd; you have to allow someone to Pastor you.

What do I mean by that? I am so very glad you asked. Shepherd can try to lead you but you must allow them to do that, you must be willing to follow. You must submit to leadership and be a faithful follower; otherwise the relationship will be of no effect.

2 Timothy 4: 2 says, **preach the word, be ready in season and out of season. Convince, rebuke, exhort with all longsuffering and teaching.**

That is the responsibility of your pastor. It is your responsibility to receive them as the one that has authority to carry this verse out in your life. You need a pastor to preach the word to you, correct you, rebuke you, deliver exhortation to you, to be long suffering, and to teach you.

In this season, having a God ordained pastoral relationship is vitally important. There are many false teachers with false doctrines. There are pastors operating in witchcraft and committing all kinds of ungodly acts.

We will get more into that in another chapter, but child of God, you must realize that God designed Shepherds; we know that God is the great Shepherd of the sheep but he called humans to serve as under Shepherds. This is definitely not the time to be without a covering.

Chapter Two:

I'm Feeling You

Your leader can feel you in the spirit.

When you have found you're ordained Pastor that was sent by God to be in your life, you become of like spirit. Your pastor will begin to feel you in the spirit because there is an attachment there. A spiritual bond has been established. The same type of attachment you have with your children your leader should now have with you. That is why they would be called not only your Shepherd or pastor but also your ***spiritual parents***, and if you allow them to Pastor and Shepherd you, you will become their "spiritual son or daughter."

Spiritual Parents

Spiritual parents are a gift directly from God. The word of God tells us that God himself gives us pastors after his own heart (Jeremiah 3:15). Your spiritual parents are your ticket to your healing, salvation, deliverance and many other mandates and needs that may arise in your life. Spiritual parents are not to replace your natural parents, yet spiritual parents are the vehicle to take you where your natural parents cannot.

As believers we have a responsibility to our leaders just as much as they have one to us. Our position is to submit to the will of God working in our leaders and allow them to mentor, impart and pull you up to the place where you need to be. Spiritual parents are not there to baby you, but rather to help you to grow and mature in the things of God. A Good leader is concerned about your growth and progression in the things of God.

One night in bible study a guest preacher at our local church gave the church an illustration of the requirements of a Bishop. He went to the scripture that says a man that desires the office of a Bishop must know how to run his own home well having his children in submission with all reverence (1 Timothy 3:5). This illustration that he gave is relevant to running the church. A church should have spiritual parents and those parents are charged with overseeing the well being of the flock. It is the responsibility of the Shepherd (spiritual parents) to do for the sheep what they cannot do for themselves, as would any good parent.

A good Shepherd knows all about his sheep. Your pastor should know when you are hurting or just going through in your spirit. Something in your leader's spirit should trigger when one of their sheep is not right, because of the spiritual connection. Jesus said he feels our infirmities, meaning, he feels what we feel, and that should be the same connection you have with your leader. It is very similar to your relationship with your own children.

A pastor should feel you in the spirit. That's why, when you leave your Shepherd's covering you immediately feel the detachment; it's like when a child leave home for college. Your pastor can feel when you are starting to disconnect yourself from the anointing. They no longer feel you. When something is wrong God is obligated to warn the Shepherd. You will begin to pull on your Shepherd's spirit and they will know that you are backsliding, they will know when you are going against them, they will know when you are getting entangled in something, they will know when you are not telling the truth, they will know when you are going through.

That is why the divine hookup is so important because if you are not divinely hooked up with your leader, they will be able to preach to you, but they will not be able to feel you in the spirit. You need to be connected in the spirit to a leader that becomes a power source. Your leader taps into the power bank of heaven making withdrawals for you and your family; you are the recipient of the divine blessing.

Jesus called the twelve men who followed him disciples. Why? When Jesus called them into his fold they stopped everything they were doing and followed him. They immediately came because they heard his voice. He knew who was supposed to be a part of his fold.

Out of those twelve he had problems with a few of them. The bible says that Peter denied him, Thomas doubted him and Judas betrayed him. The disciples also fell asleep when Jesus had asked them to stay awake and pray. Jesus knew what they were going to do when he called them because they were human, but he continued to feed them.

You may be saying I am a Peter, a Thomas or a Judas but it is still your leader's responsibility to continue to feed you. Jesus knew how to handle his sheep. When they became angry he knew how to calm them down. When they were disobedient he knew how to rebuke them. When they were in doubt he knew how to remind them of their faith. Because they were so divinely connected to Jesus he could feel them in the spirit. He knew that Peter was going to deny him and he knew Judas was going to betray him.

Jesus knew when they were getting weary in their spirits, when they were feeling sad, he just knew. How? Jesus could feel them in the spirit, he knew his sheep. The same way that Jesus knew his sheep its time the body of Christ come together in relationship with the father and without leaders getting on one accord in the spirit.

So there are going to be some bleeps and blunders? Yes, but if you know that God has called you to that fold for such a time as this,

repent and get back in place and continue to follow.

I hear the Lord saying to you, stop denying the voice of your Shepherd, stop doubting the direction your leader is taking you in, stop betraying them when things are not going well, stop falling asleep when you should be watching and praying.

Jesus continued to lead the disciples because each one had a purpose for being in that particular fold. And so do you, there is a reason that God has placed you under those particular leaders. He knows what is best for you. He knows what kind of Shepherd you need. God will place you where you belong according to the times and the seasons of your life. As long as your leader is able to feel you in the spirit, they can minister to you by the divine unction of the Holy Spirit and lead you into your destiny.

Chapter Three:

The Danger of Getting too Close

Since I have been a pastor, I have noticed that the most dangerous thing we can do as shepherds is get too close to our sheep. Your leaders have been called to lead you not to be your buddy. A lot of time this rule is broken for a various amount of reasons. As leaders, it is ok to be friendly but not to be friends. Some people feel that their leaders should also be their friends, which would be ok but as usual the enemy knows how to get in and pervert it.

As a leader **we must have boundaries**, if not the spirit of familiarity will set in. That is when you become so familiar with your leader that you no longer feel you have to obey or follow like the rest of the sheep. You begin to feel like everything the leader says does not apply to you because of the friendship. This also happens when you can no longer accept correction because you feel the leader is being biased against you because of the closeness you share.

The worst part about it is you may not realize this has happened until it is time for your leader to make a decision concerning you or they have to deliver a word to you and you feel that spirit rising up in you that says "I know they are not talking to me like that." If you find yourself in this place it's time to repent, break the flesh and bring yourself back up under submission to your leader or leaders. The worst thing you can do is kick up against the set gift that the Lord divinely put over you.

This is also true of leaders that have family members that are a part of the flock. They feel "Oh I've known Pastor since they was a baby" and they take everything as being cute or that they are doing their relative a favor by being in the fold. They feel there should be some special treatment because of familiarity.

If there is no separation in the natural, as well as in the spiritual, there is definitely going to be problems. Your leader must always be in a place they can receive respect regardless to the closeness of the relationship.

Leaders are called to go before you, not to hand out with you! So there had to be a separation, some boundaries and a difference must be set in place. Do not feel offended if you feel your leader recognizes this is happening before you do and begins to pull back. Just thank God because that is the tool the enemy uses to deceive you so that you will not receive from your leaders.

If you sense that you are getting to close to your leader or feel your leader should be your friend, remind yourself that the two cannot co-exist. You have to learn to draw the line and put your relationship with your leader in its proper place in order to gain the benefits of having a spiritual leader. While I can admit that this is not an easy road if you maintain your place and position the benefits are beautiful.

Chapter Four:

No Longer a Free Spirit

Once you come into your proper fold under your ordained Shepherd, you are no longer a free spirit. You are now tied to the spirit and vision of your leader. Your pastor is now your midwife, birthing you into your destiny.

God compares us to sheep because sheep need a Shepherd. God has given you someone now that you can be accountable to. This is the word no one likes, but we all need to be accountable to someone. Some people feel they only have to be accountable to God and that he is the only one they have to answer to. Sorry but that is not what God had in mind.

When you were a free spirit you could go from church to church (if you decided to go to church) and you had no one to answer to, no one to guide you or be accountable to, you basically did what you wanted. A free spirit allows you to make up your own rules even if they go against the word of God, after all who will know anyway. A free spirit will stay home and watch TBN on Sundays, or go to a ministry that is so big that they will not be noticed. This is all in an effort to **feel free**.

Some saints have truly been hurt by other leaders and now feel they just want to be *free* spirits. Maybe they were subject to strong spirits of control or they saw a lot of in the pulpit or the church and now they feel they do not want to put themselves through that again.

A situation like this means you were obviously under incorrect leadership.

When you are under a true Shepherd, they will have the **heart** of God and not of Pharaoh. I prophetically speak to the spirit of Pharaoh right now and I command him to "let God's people go" in Jesus name.

So whatever the reason you should no longer want to be a free spirit. Accountability is important and even in this case you will eventually start feeling unsatisfied because only whom the Son sets free is free indeed. If you are only operating as a free spirit because you are actually bound by past hurts from churches and leaders you are really not free.

It's time to embrace real leadership but even more importantly than that, it's time to embrace your deliverance.

Pray and ask the Lord to truly free you spiritually; that you may no longer operate as a free spirit but that you may be free to be in your proper fold under your divinely appointed leader. Do not allow that to continue to be a stumbling block because God desires to continue that work which he has started in you. Learn from your experiences and do not allow the enemy to lie to you anymore.

God still has a plan and purpose for you and that starts with submission and accountability. Be free in the spirit, not a free spirit.

Chapter Five:

How Do I Know When I Have Found My Shepherd?

This is a question that I have personally been asked by so many people. My answer is always the same. Let me start by telling you my own experiences since becoming a pastor.

Whenever someone comes to my ministry and I know God has called them there, it will seem as if I have seen them before, or that I actually know them from somewhere. They will also say the same thing.

After this happened a few times the Lord spoke into my spirit and said that is how you will know that I have called them to you because your spirit will already know them and their spirit will already know you.

A perfect example is in the book of Acts chapter 9 when the Lord told Ananias to go to a street called straight and find Saul, and told him that Saul had already seen him in a vision. So basically God put His plan in both of their spirits. While he was speaking to Ananias he was giving Saul the vision of who Ananias was and what he was called to do for him.

Once God establishes it in the spiritual realm, it has already happened, so when it is manifested in the natural realm it feels like you know the person or seen the person before (well you have in the spirit).

The Lord has already done it in the spirit so once you see your pastor you may not be too sure naturally but something in your spirit man will be saying "this is my pastor" and your pastor will be saying "this is one of my sheep."

Once you know that there is a divine connection between you and your leader, you are ready to become a spiritual son or daughter. Leaders should emulate the characteristics of the Holy Spirit because the Holy Spirit is a gentleman. This means he will not force himself on you. The same should be true of Gods leading men and women. You have to come to terms in yourself that you are ready to submit to the will of God for your life and render yourself under leadership.

Are you ready to become a son or daughter in Christ?

When a woman has a baby no one can breast feed that baby like the natural mother, since she is the one that originally gave birth to the child. A baby has a hard time adjusting to someone other than the mother's breast milk. The majority of the time the child will have to result to powdered milk.

When you have found your pastor, they will be able to properly feed you. But if you have not found your pastor it will feel like you are drinking powdered milk. They are preaching the word but it is not filling you up the same way it would if it were your real spiritual parents doing it. The feeding is just not satisfying.

On the flip side of that some people feel that they are not being fed but in reality they are refusing to drink. They refuse to take the feedings from the Shepherd for whatever reason. In this case Shepherds should not feel like they are doing something wrong. When I had my first son, I desired to breastfeed but he would not take it. The doctors assured me it was not my fault that some babies just refuse to drink.

In some cases there could be something wrong with the milk. Maybe the person giving it is tainting it with something else. We know in this hour we have a lot of mixed gospel going on. If that be the case, examine yourself and get back on track.

There are pastors that preach weakness, they preach that it is ok to sin that God understands or they constantly preach money, money, money, but the sheep are starving and lacking proper nourishment. Now there's nothing wrong with preaching on any specific topics, but do it by the revelation of the spirit of God and not out of the flesh. Leaders should preach a gospel with balance.

So I believe there are two ways of knowing when you have found your Shepherd. The first will be the fact that God has already done it in the spirit realm and you will get the witness in your spirit when you are faced with it in the natural realm. Sometimes this is tricky because we are led to go off emotions and what we see. God may be telling us that a Pastor Joe is the one but because he does not have a big church we will say that God could not possibly be telling us that. We cannot let self get in the way of what God is doing because of our own prejudice or issues and miss what God has for us. Believe God and let everything else be a lie. Follow your inner witness, God will deal with the rest.

God will keep confirming it in your spirit; you will find yourself thinking about his leader, you will find that you can really relate to this leader, your inner witness will keep saying this is where you belong.

The second way you will know if you have found your pastor is you will begin to be fed properly and anyone who eats well will begin to grow. So maybe you are not sure and you have never really trusted your inner witness but you find yourself getting full off the word, you are growing properly and you feel planted. The bible says in Psalm 9:14-15 tells us that we will only blossom where we are planted.

God said the day shall come when I shall bring my sheep into their proper folds. You need to pray and ask God to show you your pastor. Your life depends on it. **Stop making excuses**.

Know that your spiritual leader is sent by God to be a blessing to you.

Chapter Six:

Murmuring and Complaining

In the book of numbers we find that story of Pastor Moses a great leader called by God to lead the people into the Promise Land. But here in the 14th chapter we find the people murmuring and complaining about their present situation and began to say "let us select another leader".

That is exactly how sheep began to react when things are not going the way they planned. They begin to complain and say, "Pastor doesn't know what he/she is doing anyway." "There are always some new rules to follow."

They go as far as to say "I should have stayed at First Baptist where things were different." "We should just get somebody that knows what they are doing."

But the bible says Pastor Moses did not get upset but fell on His face right before the congregation and began to **pray** for them. Moses begins to speak to the congregation what thus saith the Lord. That means even while knowing that the congregation was talking about him and displeased with his leadership, he was still praying for them, he was still giving them the word of the Lord and concerned about them making it into the Promised Land.

Moses said, ok maybe I do not know everything but that is why I do not move unless the Lord tells me to, and I only speak what the Lord tells me to speak.

You see many people want the pastor to do what they want him to do and when he/she doesn't they began to say he does not know what he/ she is doing , but what the people do not know is that the pastor has to follow the leading of the Lord, not the people!

Moses asked the Lord, "How long will these people rebel against me? How long will they not believe in me?"The Lord told Moses to remind the people that he is a merciful God but he will not tolerate this behavior.

The people continued to talk, finally the Lord said to Moses they are not complaining against you but against **ME**. You may not know this but you are not murmuring against the pastor you are murmuring against **God.** Whenever you come against God's anointed you are coming against **God**.

Psalm 105:5 says touch not my anointed and do my prophets no harm.

The Lord spoke **judgment** over everyone that was murmuring against Moses. You see God takes it personal when you talk against the man or woman that He has sent to lead you. If you believe that your pastor is being led by God, your job is to just follow, not murmur and complain.

Because of their disobedience they were made to wander in the wilderness for 40 years. That is what will happen to you when you are complaining, you will get nowhere. You will just to in circles spiritually because you are so busy complaining you cannot see where the leaders trying to take you.

God said even some shall die in the wilderness. I hear about so many people who want to complain about their leaders, but I notice t hat they are in a dead state themselves. Spiritually they are deteriorating because they will not just FOLLOW.

You may be led to believe that you are hurting the leaders but you are just doing harm to yourself. You are causing God today I am merciful but I will not tolerate you coming against my leaders. The people are not called to correct the leaders, God is responsible for that, and all he asks you to do is follow. I always say to people if you find yourself constantly murmuring and complaining against your leader, find another ministry because you are really doing a lot of damage to yourself, for judgment is going to fall. It is safer to go where you can respect your leader.

If there is something that is being said or done that is not right God will deal with the leader. **Keep your mouth off of them. I repeat keep your mouth off of them**. Take this as a warning. If you have been guilty of doing this, **"STOP"**. You may feel God has not done anything to me yet, well maybe he gave you another chance for you to read this and repent. Remember God told Moses to warn them again before he sent destruction.

In verse 37 it says that even those that brought back the evil report died by a plague sent from the Lord. Even if you are not the one slandering the leader, do not be a bearer of evil reports either. Do not even sit in the company of those that are slandering the leaders, get away from them quickly. Before you do, make sure you let them know that God is not pleased with that type of behavior and will soon judge them for their acts. Get with those sheep that are celebrating your leader, stay away from those that are cursing them and being a stumbling block to the vision.

Pastors teach on this subject all the time and no matter how you say it or teach it, people continue to do it, not realizing that there is a high price to pay for disobedience.

I know I speak for so many leaders when I say this; you have to learn to pray for your leader and stop murmuring and complaining. You need to say this to yourself over and over, I will pray for my leader.

Chapter Seven:

Get in the Ark of Safety

There are times when God will only speak to the Leader. If you are truly a follower and disciple, whenever your leader speaks, because you have relationship with the Lord and are in divine connection with your leader everything God says to your leader should be confirmation.

Noah was also a type of Pastor. In the book of Genesis when God was ready to send the flood He told Noah to preach. Note here that He told only Noah what was going to happen, not the people. In Genesis 6:14 it says "and God said unto Noah."

There will be times when God will only speak through the leader and you will have to listen and get in the ark of safety. Whether it is not to marry a certain person, or not to get entangled with certain things, listen! They are trying to keep you in the ark of safety.

We see here that God was talking to the people but telling Noah what to say to the people. I can hear the saying, "Noah does not know what he's talking about if God was going to destroy us he would tell us himself." But if they were in connection with God Noah's message should have been confirmation for them or they should have been able to act out of obedience even if they did not understand, because they trust Noah as a true man of God.

Know that there will be plenty of times that your leader will hear God for you, when God is talking about you, but not to you. In order to receive from your leader what God is trying to deposit into you, you must receive your leader as a gift from God as they operate on your behalf.

Not listening to your leader can mean **life** or **death** for you. I know so many Pastors who preach and preach and preach but people do not listen and then when the flood in their life comes, they are overtaken.

Don't let it be said to late once the flood comes it's too late. Listen to your Noah and get in the Ark of safety now!

Chapter Eight:

Until Death Do Us Part

I sincerely believe that a Shepherd/sheep relationship is until death do us part. I believe it is a lifelong connection that is to be only separated by death.

There was no permanent separation between Jesus and his disciples until Jesus died on the cross and even then Jesus said I will not leave you comfortless but I will leave my spirit to be with you. And they continued to preach what Jesus (their leader) taught them.

There was no permanent separation between Elijah and Elisha until Elijah went to be with the Lord and Elisha received his mantle. Everything that Elijah taught him he was now able to use in his ministry. He operated under the teaching of his leader Elijah.

When you find your pastor it should be until death do us part. You are there until death or the rapture, whichever comes first. There is no reason to leave your covering and the place that God has called you to. Even if God elevates you into your own ministry that is still your Shepherd, your leader, and you're covering. You have just changed levels spiritually.

Your parents will always be your parents. It is the same with your spiritual parents. After you grow up and leave home naturally your parents will always be your parents you are just all grown up and living somewhere else. Everything your parents taught you, you will now exemplify in your own home. When it's time for you to step out, you will have grown, and will be able to stand on your own, you will be well taught and able to handle your won house (ministry) well.

Of course things happen where you may have to leave your covering. God may have ordained for you to be with a particular leader but it can be turned around, not on God's part but the sheep or Shepherd can do something or allow something to come in between the plan of God. We can mess up our own blessings.

God can ordain you to be with a Shepherd and then that Shepherd begins to fall into sin, or began to spiritually abuse and neglects the sheep. Or the sheep can become disobedient to the shepherd without repentance and have to be excommunicated from the ministry. For those that been hurt by leadership and you left your covering for that reason, I believe what happens is, you are placed in foster care. God places you where you can be fed and taken care of until you are ready and can handle permanent placement again.

I have seen children turned over to foster care because of the devastation of what happened with their biological parents. A lot of these children go from foster home to foster home because they become rebellious. Sheep will go from church to church because they have been hurt, and they will not let God heal them if their pain. **God desired to heal you**, he may have placed you somewhere safe that you may heal and learn how to love and trust again and then He will prepare your heart for permanent placement again.

God may place you in a ministry where you will feel safe, it will feel ok, and the word will be good, the spiritual parents are nice but you know that it is not your permanent place. God does this so that you may heal and realize that all leaders are not the same. There are some real men and women that have been called by God and will in no means abuse or neglect you.

Some sheep are able to make the adjustment immediately and go right into permanent placement again but be careful of going on your own, follow the leading of the Holy Spirit.

Sometimes you may be fearful and unsure of whom to trust and where to go so let God lead you.

Sheep can also mess up with whom God places them with. They become deceived by the enemy through betrayal, as did Judas. Judas betrayed Jesus for 30 pieces of silver. Jesus forgave him but Judas decided to commit suicide (again you are only hurting yourself). You may be forgiven but now your leader is not able to trust you. This eventually leads to a separation, usually because, like Judas, the person cannot forgive themselves.

As a pastor, I have personally had to bring correction to some of my sheep and finally after not seeing any repentance, I would have to ask them to remove themselves from the fellowship so they will hopefully come to a point of repentance. This is after knowing that the lord sent them to sit under my leadership. You may not agree and say if the Lord sent them to you, as a shepherd you have no right to release them but when Adam and Eve was in the garden it was not God's will to cast them out but Eve decided to eat the forbidden fruit, the same thing God told them not to do they did.

Titus 3: 10-11 A man that is a cause of divisions, after admonishing him a first and second time, reject him from your fellowship and have nothing more to with him.

The scriptures clearly tell us here that as shepherds we have to know when we have warned enough and now this person is becoming dangerous to the other sheep. There are some situations that we as shepherds cannot tolerate, for in doing so may tarnish the rest of the fold. Yes, excommunication is in the word, we are going to see the difference in the flock.

God desires for you to stay with the leader he had placed you under, and when He does stay faithful and obedient until you grow up and leave home or until he calls you home.

Chapter Nine:

When Should I Leave a Church or Ministry?

This is another question asked by so many. As I mentioned in the previous chapter, you should not leave your covering, it is until death do you part. But know what I am talking about healthy relationships. When you know that you have found your covering and God has without a shadow of a doubt placed you under that particular Shepherd, **you basically have no reason to leave.**

I believe God has a time and place for everything. For when time and place meet you have **destiny**. Some people feel I can go to any church; But God has a specific place for you to be and a time for you to be there.

Again if you have found that place do not move unless God says so. And the question is how do I know if God is telling me to leave?

I truly believe there are only 3 reasons you should leave a church or ministry. My beliefs are based on the word of God.

1.) When there is sin coming from the leadership that is not being corrected or there is no repentance. (Even **compromise** is sin.)

When God spoke to the Angels of the church (the leaders) in the book of revelation he would first compliment them and then tell them what He had against them. If you are sitting under someone who is living in sin and not repenting (e.g. pastor sleeping with the members of the church) or even allowing others to sin knowingly and not bring correction that is compromise, God says in Rev. 2:16 "repent unless I come to you quickly." I recommend if you see no repentance get out.

You will be judged on what you know. You have not been called to change anyone; the Holy Spirit has to do the changing. Do not be deceived and allow the enemy to tell you that you have no right to judge anyone, but the bible judges them all by itself, sin is sin no matter who it come from so if they are in sin the bible say they are a sinner and God judges all sin.

Paul says we are to judge those who are within the church. Know that you are judging the actual sin (the act) not the person.

2.) If you are not being fed. (Remember discern if you are not being fed because the shepherd is not feeding you properly or are you refusing to drink).

It is the shepherd's responsibility to feed the sheep. You should also leave if there is abuse coming from the Shepherd. I stand strongly on this. But you must know the difference between abuse and correction.

In the book of Ezekiel chapter 34 the Lord says, "**Woe to the Shepherds who feed themselves, Behold I am against those shepherds, the shepherds fed themselves and not my flock, they scattered because there was no shepherd."**

Here we find the lord speaking against those shepherds who did **not feed the sheep nor heal those that were sick, nor bind up the broken, but ruled with force and cruelty, and because of that the sheep scattered.** Which mean the sheep left the fold because they were not being fed.

3.) Another reason would be if God has elevated you into a ministry that causes you to be absent from your leader such as becoming a pastor, evangelist or missionary work. (Even then it is done with decency and in order.)

You do not leave your ministry because of offense. **Most of the time people will say they are leaving for one of the reasons above but in reality they are leaving because they are offended by something that was said or done.**

As Christians we must realize that offenses will come but we must know how to handle it and we must be convinced in our hearts that offenses will not move us out of our divine place. Just because the pastor did something you did not agree with (but it was not sin) for instance he decided to take down the curtains you bought and replace them with new ones and you feel offended, is not a reason to leave your place.

The enemy loves offense because he uses that as a tool to get you to turn against your leader and when that takes place you immediately stop receiving from your leader which stunts your growth and causes you to move out of your place prematurely. He will begin to deceive you into thinking your leaders are trying to poison you and that they are out to get you.

The enemy knows how to get you to leave your covering; he knows how to orchestrate things and get you to believe your leader is in error. He wants to get you from underneath your covering so he can have a field day with you.

Never walk in offense against your leaders, it is dangerous. Offense causes you to see things that are not happening, or there may be some issues that the enemy will magnify and blow up to be bigger than it really is. You will even hear things that were not really said. It will cause you not to see spiritually because offense brings on the attitudes of the flesh. (See 2 Co. 2:14-15)

Proverbs 18:19 **A brother offended is harder to be won than s strong city, and their contentions separate them like the bars of a cast**. (Amplified Bible)

I have dealt with people who became offended over something that happened in the ministry and all of a sudden they come to the church with attitudes, they are making faces while you are preaching, they start poisoning the other sheep, and they start making excuses to miss church.

As a shepherd, you know when one of your sheep is trying to leave because they have been offended; it becomes obvious in their behavior. A Shepherd is responsible for bringing restitution to the situation, not just allow the sheep to wander. Sometimes this doesn't work because the sheep have their mind made up they are offended and tend to stay that way. In that regards, there is nothing the shepherd can do.

It is very hard for shepherds to contend with those sheep that refuse to just **let it go and grow**. As a sheep you should make up your mind that offenses will come but when they do, I will make it my business to get it straight and move on.

Also the shepherd knows when the sheep has been elevated by God and it is time for them to move on. The Shepherd should then be willing to release the sheep with their blessings. This also does not always work out this way, sometimes the shepherd is not willing to allow them to go when it is time, but if you have truly heard from the Lord and know that he is say it's time to move on, be obedient to the Lord and not man. (Again this calls for discernment, you have to know that God is saying this, because God is a God of order he will let your leader know that he has called you and there is a work to do.) Do not just step out on your own, **but also do not sit somewhere and die or forfeit the call of God on your life.**

Do not be afraid to leave a ministry if God is telling you to. So many people stay in places where they are bound up, and they are not being fed so they are not growing spiritually, they also have calls on their lives but they refuse to move.

I thank God that I have true understanding of the sheep/shepherd relationship. As a shepherd there are times when you have to say this person is not growing in my ministry, maybe it is time for them to move on and you must be willing to let them do just that. If you are a leader and you are reading this, ask God to help you in this area, because it is important to know who God has assigned to be in your ministry, when to release them, and when it is time for them to just move on. You should not try to hold people in your ministry because of your own selfish reasons.

And if you are a sheep reading this, know that you cannot go to hell for leaving one ministry and going to another ministry. Yes, you are still saved. And if you feel the Lord telling you to move (for the right reason) trust Him to lead you and direct your path.

Chapter Ten:

Concern or Control

I am a pastor and I'm also a seer. This can be very challenging because sometimes I see more that I desire to see and know more that I desire to know. As a pastor with the heart of God I am genuinely concerned for my sheep. As a sheep you must understand that it is your shepherd's job to protect you at all costs. You must also understand the difference between concern and control.

You can tell which spirit is under operation by watching the motive of the leader. Everything you ever need to know about what a person is doing is wrapped up in their intention. Pray and ask God for discernment in your life so you can see people for who they are, that includes your leader. Once you know the spirit of you leader you will not have a problem submitting and being led. You will also know if a leader is operating out of another spirit.

When leaders operate under a spirit of control that spirit has a **selfish motive**, something about is benefits them. They are trying to control you for their own purposes. For example, when a leader tells someone that they cannot go to the mall, because it is a sin; something like that is considered control. Now going to the mall is not a sin but because of their own beliefs they will try to control you and stop you from going.

When leaders operate out of concern it benefits the sheep. If a leader tells his sheep "try not to go to the mall late at night because there have been a lot of robberies there lately." That is not control; that is concern.

If the leader says to you "the young man you are dating is not for you" Instead of getting upset and saying they are just trying to control me being to say, "my leader must see something I do not see." Ask yourself the question who is this benefiting?

My husband and I had this situation occur early in our ministry. There was a young lady coming to our ministry professing salvation, married to one man but living with another man. One Sunday the Lord spoke through my husband to tell this young lady that this situation was not of God and this was a warning to her. Well she told us right to our face that she was going to continue to pray for the relationship to work anyways. My husband said a feeling came over him that he could not explain, he said "she thinks she is hurting us but she is really slapping God in the face." we could do nothing bow by pray, but we knew she was sitting in judgment.

Basically she was telling us "you can't tell me what to do, nobody is going to control me." This young lady never returned to the church and within a few weeks returned to her former life of drugs and alcohol, and that same man she was praying for married someone else. We were telling her exactly what the Lord was saying to her in line with the word of God.

That is why you must know the spirit of your leader. **1 John 4:1 says believe not every spirit, but test the spirits to see if it is from God**. Ask the Lord to show you the spirit of your leader and He will. God will show you if they have a controlling spirit (and if they do run for the border) a controlling spirit is considered to be a form of witchcraft.

But if your leader has a proven track record of seeing in the spirit and shows concern for your soul, become submissive and obedient to the wisdom and knowledge of your leader.

I totally disagree when people say certain sheep/shepherd relationships are cultish in nature. People do not get me wrong there are some that really are. But we cannot say that in all cases, there are some situations where more attention must be given to the sheep. For instance, when someone first gets saved the pastor must take more time with them. They usually have a lot of questions and are in need of direction. So in the beginning the pastor may be a hands-on mentor, it may look like they go to the pastor for everything, the pastor is always telling them what to do, but that is because they are a babe in Christ and babes are at a stage where the parent has to do what they are not capable of doing. If the person happens to not be a babe they may be dealing with some serious personal situations of crisis or deliverance. In that case it's nobody's business what they go to the pastor for.

As time goes by the sheep should be growing and able to do more and more independently with maturity and wisdom. After a certain time the leader should be teaching the disciple to do a mature Christian, no longer need the same attention. Sometimes a Shepherd may do this to keep the sheep under a spirit of control.

When a shepherd is truly concerned he will teach them to grow in the Lord. Remember, your leader sees what you do not see, so maybe you think it is control but in the long run it will benefit you.

Again the story of Noah, I am quite sure the people thought, "Oh boy here goes Noah again trying to tell us what to do." But the truth of the matter is He was trying to keep them from dying. The bible records no one was saved but Noah and his family. They thought Noah was operating under a spirit of control instead of concern.

Let's tell the truth and shame the devil; no one likes to be told what to do. There is something in all of us that says "can't no body tell me what to do but God." Oh foolish Christians how easily deceived. Whenever God is speaking through your leader that is God (please note I said when God is speaking). Believers need to understand that the voice of your leader is the voice of God. Your leader is not a God to you, but he/she is the voice of God to you. Count yourself blessed to be under a leader who is concerned about your wellbeing.

Yes, it is a blessing to know that someone cares about whether you live or die. They are concerned if you are in an unhealthy relationship. They are concerned if you may be hanging around people that are bringing you down. I am going to ask you right now that if you know you have a concerned leader to **lift your hands and begin to praise God** for the gift that He has placed in your life, just begin to count your blessings.

If you have a selfish, controlling, manipulative, Jezebelish leader hear God and live, run for the border. Some may not agree and say No, they should pray but I say pray from a distance and get to a place of safety and remove yourself from that spirit of witchcraft.

Chapter Eleven:

Am I Guilty of Shepherd Abuse?

While there is so much talk about sheep abuse there is also a lot of shepherd abuse going on as well. The bible gives many accounts on how the shepherd should treat the sheep and also how the shepherd should respond to the sheep. When these biblical principles are followed, then I believe the plan God designed for the relationship will be a blessing to all parties involved.

How can I be guilty of shepherd abuse? Most of us tend to think that our leaders are not human, that they have no feelings. Please get that thought out of your mind, because it is simply not true. We hurt, we cry, we get angry, we feel sad, and we get disappointed just like you do. The same things that hurt you hurt us.

The bible says you should treat others, as you also want to be treated that include your relationships with your leader. Sheep tend to think that they can treat their leaders any kind of way and say all types of hurtful things and it takes no affect on their leader.

Well I come to let you know that is not true!

Proverbs 18:21 Death and life are in the power of the tongue. Stop killing your pastor with your tongue. Instead bring life to them by encouraging them with your words.

It hurts to know that your disciples are somewhere in deep ungodly conversations about you, that they are undermining everything that you are trying to do. It disappoints leaders when you betray them and turn your back on them. When you spread vicious lies about your leaders that make them cry. When you are causing division among the brethren and sowing seeds of discord we become sad and sometimes angry.

Any type of mistreatment that has a negative effect on someone can be considered abuse. You do not have to physically hit someone for it to be abuse; there is verbal abuse. Verbal abuse is where a person uses words to hurt another person.

We cannot forget spiritual abuse where it basically tears down your spirit man. You can no longer function spiritually because of the hurt and pain being caused by another person.

I have heard countless stories of shepherd abuse and have seen so many shepherds that are no longer shepherding because of this.

Please don't be guilty of this; love your leader, appreciate them, honor them, uphold them because that is what you want in return. We always say do unto others as we would have done to ourselves and here is your opportunity to do right. Start with your leader. Honor love and cherish them as a gift that God has set over your life.

Chapter Twelve:

No Dogs Allowed!

Philippians 3:2 Beware of dogs, beware of evil workers of confusion.

One night I had a dream that I was surrounded by barking dogs. I was standing in the middle and the dogs were all around me barking very loud and ferociously.

One of the dogs particularly kept trying to grab hold of my clothes; I was not fearful but concerned about not getting bit by any of these dogs. Right away I knew this was a God given dream. I began to pray and ask the Lord to give me the interpretation.

The spirit of the Lord took me to the book of **Matthew 7:6 "do not give what is holy to the dogs, nor cast your pearls before swine, lest they trample them under their feet and turn and tear you in pieces."**

As I began to do some research I found out that dogs and pigs serve together as a picture of what is vicious, unclean and abominable.

Dogs can be so disgusted that they can turn on their master. So the scripture forbids proclaiming the sacred gospel of the kingdom to certain people designed as dogs and pigs.

Dogs and pigs refer to anyone who has given clear evidences of rejecting the gospel with vicious and hardened attempt. Meaning they give all clear signs that they do not really want to be saved. The part the Holy Spirit focused me in on was the fact that you could be an owner of dog for a very long time, feeding him very well, taking him for walks; he may even sleep in the same bed as you do. But one day this dog that portrays himself as a man's best friend, can be licking your face and out of the clear blue become frustrated and angry for any reason and just turn on you.

I have seen it happen, someone I knew owned a pit bull for over 6 years, they fed him, walked him, and he played with the kids, but one day he just turned on the owner, and today he has lost one of his arms because of this dog. What we do not understand is that is the nature of a dog, at any given time a dog can turn on you. When people say, "My dog doesn't bite," I say to myself he may never have bitten anyone before but that is his nature.

When we take a closer look at this revelation, that is how a spirit of rebellion operates it gets angry and revolts. As shepherds we have to be aware of dogs. It may sound cruel but that is the truth. They were pretending to be harmless but waiting for the right moment to attack. They may look like sheep but inwardly be raging wolves. You have to kick up your discernment and be ready at all times for what may present itself.

Dogs are naturally rebellious that is why you have to train them. When we have them as pets we try to train them not to bite or be vicious unless they feel their owner is in danger. But because of the spirit of rebellion they may just turn on the exact one they are supposed to be protecting.

Rebellion raises its head unexpectedly, you really do not know someone is rebellious until you say something they do not like or agree with. And even then they will start out by just barking. **Shepherds beware of the bark.** In the book of Psalms it say, **"they growl like a dog, swords are in their lips, they go all around the city and howl if they are not satisfied."**

These are the one that do not agree with something and instead of dealing with it the proper way, they start going around telling everybody they want to leave the church. That is when the start going around telling people that there is something wrong with the church and spreading lies and their own selfish opinions. I heard a saying once "a dog's bark can be louder that his bite." And yes, sometimes the barking can be enough.

The dogs are the same ones that you spend most of your time feeding and nurturing and then for no apparent reason, they being to bark at you know that it will not be long before you feel the bite. Use your prophetic senses and know that following the bark, may lead to a bite. You have the time to lead the situation another direction before the bite takes place. That's right it will not be long before they get tired of barking and just decide to attack.

Well as they do in the natural if a dog attacks someone they put him to sleep. If you have been bitten put that spirit of rebellion to sleep. Kill it in your church; let the sheep know that it will not be tolerated. My husband who is also my spiritual covering said to me, "as a pastor God has called you to feed sheep, not goats, pigs or dogs. Let them know you only have sheep food, not dog food."

Make it known "No Dogs Allowed!"

This is the spirit that attacks the shepherd the most. The spirit of rebellion is prevalent in many churches. It's time to break the spirit of rebellion, expose it where ever you find it. Rebellion is not a spirit you counsel or handle in private. Rebuke them openly so others may fear. Lead them to repentance if they will repent. If not rebuke and cast out that spirit before it ravages your ministry.

Chapter Thirteen:

Whose report will you believe?

Jeremiah was a prophet from his mother's womb, also called to be a pastor to the people of God. As a pastor and prophet, Jeremiah has a very tough assignment. He was often called the weeping prophet. The Lord used him to warn the people of coming judgment for their sins.

Pastor Jeremiah was truly a man that spoke what thus saith the Lord. In the 17th chapter the people began to say where is the word of the Lord? In other words everything that you were prophesying, when is it going to come to pass? In other words let's see it Pastor Jeremiah. I can imagine they begin to mock the words of the prophet.

That is equivalent to the true prophets and pastors of today. Often we are mocked because of the words that the Lord is giving to his prophets today. There is definitely a trumpet being blown in Zion saying prepare ye the way of the Lord, but the people are saying when is it going to happen?

Pastor Jeremiah began to plead his case before the Lord; He said "Lord I still did not stop being a shepherd to your people even after they were coming up against me and calling me a false prophet, because I know you called me to this assignment, you ordained me from my mother's womb, and I never preached or prophesied anything that you did not give me."

That is how we must be as pastors and prophets of today. We must learn to stand our ground no matter if they receive it or not. The results are not our responsibility, that part belongs to the Lord. We must cry loud and spare not. We have to understand when your fulfilling your God assignment not everyone will be happy about it or much less receptive of it. You have to begin to rest in your assignment and avoid adapting to the mindset of the people around you or if they receive your ministry or word from the Lord.

Jeremiah began to pray in verse 18 that the people would be dismayed and receive double destruction. (Note he did not curse the, leaders should not curse anyone that is not our place that is witchcraft). But God told him to warn them again and if they did not listen he will send destruction.

Sheep must understand that is the character of God. He is a loving and merciful God and will continue to warn and give chances but if the prophet of God says "the Lord is going to do thus and thus for your disobedience." The pastor or prophet is not being mean or cursing you. He is peaking what thus saith the Lord. If the Lord tells the leader to warn you that is that he has to do. The bible says it is better to obey God than man.

In the book of Ezekiel chapter 3 the Lord gave Ezekiel strict instructions about his ministry.

He said, "I have made you a watchman, therefore hear the words of my mouth and give them a warning for me. When I say to the wicked you shall surely die and you give him no warning and he dies in his iniquity, I will require the blood at your hands, but if you warn the wicked and he chooses not to turn from his wicked ways you have delivered your soul.

Basically we are responsible to tell the sheep whatever God tells us, but the results are not up to us (thank you Jesus). We can all accept a word from the pastor or prophet when they are telling us we are about to get a new house, or a new car, but what about when the Lord tells them to tell us to get the sin out of our lives, or when the Lord tells him to tell you that your motives are not pure.

As a pastor and prophet I have had to give many prophetic words. Some were good; some were not so good, but I make sure that I do not speak unless I am under the divine unction of the Holy Spirit.

I have also learned that you can give the same advice to two people facing a familiar situation and one will love you for it and the other will hate you for it. Why? When you experience this don't blame or beat up yourself, because the issue was not in your advice, but in who they were. Know that it's not that your pastor is giving you a false word, you need to check yourself and see if your flesh just wants to rebel against the advice given. If the enemy gets a whiff of this he knows exactly what to do.

That's right; send you a false prophet with a false word. Most sheep would quickly receive a word from someone other than their leader, because they feel their leader already knows so much about them. Well that is why God would tell them first, a stranger does not know your spirit but your leader does. Because God is a God of order anything a prophet tells you should be confirmation to you and your leader.

So many people have grab hold of prophetic words from others and totally dismissed the word from the one that sees with the eyes of the spirit for them. Always line the prophetic word up with the word of God. God is not going to do anything outside of his word. As I said I also operate in the prophetic, if God says anything he will definitely back it with his word. For Jesus said in Matthew 24:35. **"Heaven and earth will pass away but my words will by no means pass away."**

Speaking as a prophet and pastor, please run all prophetic words by your pastor to be judged accordingly, for many false prophets are running about in the land. While it may sound old school and people may even be saying "who does that?" it will protect you from unnecessary pitfalls. That's what your shepherd is there for, to help you sift through things in life, their job is to keep you on a straight path.

In Jeremiah 27:9-10 it says "therefore do not listen to your prophets, diviners, dreamers, soothsayers and sorcerers who say to you," you shall not serve the king of Babylon, for they prophesy lies to you to remove you from your land" (dreams, meaning your own dreams or the dream of others, we must be careful also of our own dreams). Be prayerful and watchful, some prophecies come to move you out of your place.

What do you mean Pastor? Well the enemy knows how to say the right words, give you the right dreams; actually the enemy knows just what you want to hear that will get you out of your place in God. You must guard your spirit to be sure that you don't develop itching ears. There are false prophets who will come to you prophesying exactly what you want to hear, moving you away from the purpose of what God has for you. Then there are some prophets who are not seasoned in their gift and will prophesy something to you that will lead you off course and can have a damaging effect on your life.

For example, I have seen prophets come and prophesy to women that they need to prepare themselves for God is getting ready to send them a husband. Despite the fact their pastor has told them that the Lord wants them to focus on their relationship with Him, but as I said we are more likely to listen to a stranger that is telling us what we want to hear. Before they received the word they were doing just that seeking God and growing spiritually. But upon hearing this word they no longer attend bible study, now they are running from church to church looking for this husband.

They begin taking it upon themselves to look for a man when the man should be finding them correct? They are even looking at one of their brother's friend who is not saved but is showing an interest in them. And when the pastor tries to bring correction, they feel the pastor is being controlling, but in reality they know and see through the spirit where this road is going to lead them. Before long that person is out the door with some controlling, abusive, alcoholic for a husband. I have seen this happen time and time again.

Beware, Beware, Beware of false prophets!

I believe the people of God need to be taught how to deal with the prophetic. You have to know that because your pastor knows your spirit he may not be a prophet but God can use him to give you the word of wisdom. Do not take a strangers word over your leader's word. Trust your leader first and foremost.

Your leader is going to help you get your inheritance. The bible says your inheritance is amongst those who are sanctified. Whatever you need, God puts it in your leader. When you can begin to see that from a spiritual standpoint, you will stop all disloyalty, disobedience and rebellion and allow the Holy Spirit that abides in your leader to ride you into your inheritance and destiny.

Remember we are not talking about soulish leadership in this book, but we are referring to Leaders that have been called by God, walking in a true anointing, being led by the Holy Spirit, and operating in love with the heart and mind of God. This type of leader is worthy of Double Honor.

Chapter Fourteen:

The Final Chapter

I say this to all that has gotten this far in your reading. I decided to let this be the final chapter. In an all out effort to get the message across to both shepherds and the sheep, there are some things that are just not going to happen until that shepherd/sheep relationship is biblically correct.

Beloved, your ministry cannot even take off until you get in your proper place. You may not believe that God has a set man/woman that is going to get you where he needs you to be and kicking against the pricks just prolongs the process.

Let's refer to Pastor Moses again. If the people would have just listened and obeyed, they could have made it to the promise land but was delayed and they were made to wander for 40 years. Some of you are delaying your own process by not being obedient. God has told you what to do but you are kicking against the voice of God. Do not let the devil do that to you. The devil's plan is to take an event and establish a cycle in your life so that you can never be satisfied and connected anywhere, to any church, or to any pastor. Do not let that vagabond spirit control your life. Get delivered from the Cain spirit (wandering spirit).

You can be committed to a church and to a pastor. Command that tormenting spirit to flee from you in Jesus name. If the enemy is trying to keep you out the church, you continue to go in. You are called to be a tree planted by the waters not tumbleweed. When you are planted in a house, you will be able to attach yourself to the vision. You will begin to flourish in the things of God.

They (the children of Israel) also were a people who talk too much. As you are following your leader, study to be quiet. This may come as a hard thing for some of us, but that is going to be the key to your next level in God. My grandmother used to say, "It is better to eat too much than to talk too much". The next time you feel yourself getting ready to talk, go eat a piece of bread instead!

I encourage you to find your shepherd, seek out your pastor; your next level depends on it. Remove all hindrances and stumbling blocks and get in the place God has ordained for you to be in. If you know that you have not found that designated place, you are missing the blessings God has in store for you. If you are in your designated pace, I encourage you to stay where you are, bless God for this season in your life, and continue to grow in the Lord.

Shepherds I pray that you continue to feed the flock that God has assigned to you with all love and concern, and if you have not been doing so that you will start as of this day, knowing that you have to answer to God for all things.

1 Peter 5:2 tells us to "shepherd the flock which is among you, serving as overseers, not by the constraint but willingly not for dishonest gain but eagerly."

Let us prepare for the return of our soon coming King. Yes he is coming back again and real soon. For in the book of revelation Jesus says **"behold I come quickly and my reward is with me, to give to everyone according to his work.**

It behooves you to live a holy and righteous life. This is not the time to allow your pride to keep you from hearing the spirit of the Lord in this hour. Put pride under arrest right now, for that is the main reason why we do not obey, we allow pride to get in the way.

Jesus said He is coming back for a church without a spot or wrinkle. And you are the church, not the building that you attend every Sunday.

> Ephesians 5:27 Says, **"That He might present himself a glorious church, not having a spot or wrinkle or any such thing, but that it should be holy and without blemish."**

We are in a strategic time when we have no choice but to be obedient to the voice of the Lord and obey his commandments. Ask the Lord to fine-tune your ear that you may hear what the Lord is saying to you, it's time to move into the will of God for your life NOW.

My prayer is that this book has ministered to your heart on the importance of a shepherd and sheep relationship; that you will begin to receive the relationship in your spirit that God has divinely appointed with you and your leader or with you and your sheep. My prayer is also that you will see all that God intends for you to see.

To God's most precious people, God has placed the shepherd in your life as the one who sees in the spirit for you, so lie down in green pastures and rest in the Holy Spirit. Shepherds of the Most High God; know that you have been called to see in the spirit for the sheep and as of this day be honored that you have been chosen to be a vessel in this last and final hour.

Other Books by the Author

Dr. Michelle Davis is also the other of:

1. There is no Weapon Woman warfare manual: Released: 2005
2. Seeing with the eyes of the Spirit: Released: 2007
3. Behind Closed Doors: Scheduled Release 2012

Notes:

www.ingramcontent.com/pod-product-compliance
Lightning Source LLC
LaVergne TN
LVHW020650100826
845148LV00012B/2422

9780615809182